Wrecked Looking Glass

Lena Saunders

BookLeaf
Publishing

Presentation by *BookLeaf Publishing*

Web: www.bookleafpub.com

E-mail: info@bookleafpub.com

ISBN: 9789357214346

First edition 2023

Thanks to Professor for always believing in me.

Thank you PeeWee and Johnny D Malugin for finding me and giving me guidance when I found little.

Thank you mom for investing in me with full belief of a success story.

Thanks to Dani Krisp and Kristie Thomas for showing your constant love and support.

Because of all you I was able to believe in myself enough to finally go for it. Muwah

Decisions

Taking steps forward to walk through a door of an unknown is scary to say the least. Who are we if not people who see future in eyes of hope for a better way. Trying is success even if the effort seemed mundane, more or less.

Take a thousand steps forward, take a thousand more if that's what it has to be. Failure is not achieving the goal first, second or third attempt. Failure is when we quit, give up, show no more care, watch on side line with a muzzle on your voice.

We all have a reason to walk the earth. We all have the rights to be just who you choose to be. In uniting the strength of many can bring justice and less victimizing.

I have been in a place where I don't want to walk out my door for days, I cry, I sing, I laugh at how silly I am being. Standing up and stepping forward takes will to live. Our hearts lead a majority count....our hearts are weak and are easily fooled. Our hearts have soul and can be darken as well as bring light. Our choices bring the next chapters of life. I made the choices that brought me to my victimizing. I showered myself in gloomies and self pity.

Now looking in the mirror, I decide to be my own hero, be my own person with out fear to live. I decide I have more inside me to keep walking my path. I decide today is my turn to fight for myself and my purpose given. This is yet a mystery my purpose here...I do believe I have more love in me than I can hold. I have a mind that grows with each word in a sentence read. This life has mountains of learning and finding ways to feel you belong.

I make the decision to fight for Humanity, fight for Unity, fight for standing up for what's Right...gray zone is still a zone to stand for as is for the weak and strong...the victims and predators.

Every life matters every life was born for a reason...stand up and fight for the purpose of why we were created and brought forth.

Love more...care more....laugh more....cry more. Mostly, just make a decision!

Darling Friend

Darling Friend

Lean on me
Let mine carry thee
This feeling is fleeting
It cuts deep with heavy bleeding
Dearest friend of mine
Let go of your tight grip
Let me mend your hearts rip
Lean on me
Let mine carry thee
Find with me a cain
To walk you thru the darkest rain
Blue is a serinity color
Green is with fierce desire
Purple will subdue a calm in you
Take my hand I hold out
Let's both go scream and shout
Howl out to our moons shadowed self
Darlin in time this oneside drout will be felt
deep
Pedistooled in loving memory
Framed and set on a shelf
Lean on me
Let mine carry thee

My brave delicate friend
Let me tell you
Everything will be ok

More Humanity

Will not stand silent when disrespectful behavior
turns their ugly scowls at me.

I will not be the doormat for vultures to peck at
my forgiving kindness. It's easy for me to
forgive people who has sincere expressed energy

This carries me thru knowing my heart continues
to be warm and caring. Rather than cold and
shut off.

I give opportunities for riteousness to be upheld.
There is no wrong moment to start being a better
person with pure intentions and loving more.

Profound as it sounds, humanity can still come
back from the evil restraints built from all the
chaos and one man for themself attitude.

We are humans weak to our emotional and
mental states of mind and greed for more,
More money
More power
More love
More gadgets and gizmos

More needs
More fake persauds
More vulnerable to the devil's leaking venom of
riches of plenty, fame to many, and manipulation
to do his dirty deeds.

Humans empathetic tendencies and morality
render us weakest species of all Gods creation.

Taking advantage of us who have huge hearts
with the aim to bring life back to our country,
bring back "We the People" is the kink that has
us all ready to sink.

I am ME... I am forgiving, I am caring, I am
giving, I rarely think of myself, I rarely do for
myself. More do I remember doing for
ungrateful others than do I recall ungrateful
others ever attempting to do for me.

Sad sad sad realization!
I will hold true to what is my cores glue.
It's what holds me steady to manage my skipped
beats

I am a healer with mind waves crashing in and
wrapping the pains in the tunnels to allow them
to roll away all over the oceans bay.

To be a good person, one should give another the chance to change up and do different. Believe in them and there goodside before slashing and lashing, scolding their molding.

This is the freedom of choices. This is faulting and dustructive. Giving so easily makes me an easy target.

No more! Won't let it, won't take it, Won't fake it, won't belittle my graceful taste to believe there is good in our human race. Maybe we just need to smack some in the face.

I will always hold myself accountable and take what comes to me if I step out of my mending ways. Showing someone their ugly ass ways. Bullies and no good doers, theives and many yucky muck others will account for theirs, if not from me, then karma's shadow will creep in and hulk smash them down deep. Bluntly force them to mend their wicked ways.

I will be karma soon. That day people will wish they cared more!

Not Lost

Peterpan let's go be lost in the land of the free.
Where leaves of many shower thier skittled
colors all around.
Jump into piles of many.
We can rush in to oceans so blue, let the waves
crash into our playful hold.
Folding us in blankets of seaweed and sandmans
soft lands.
Tell me can we even be lost in mountains capped
in iced blue where your breath sees cycles too?
Man would be ever so grand to really tour our
land. Getting lost is not getting lost if you have
no destination in plan.
Yes please let's go get completely lost in the seas
of plenty.
Let's find this special place we have been
destined for.
Not our plan, this is the divine plan.
We can feast on the berry's and build fires that
glow ever warm.
Dance under the stars and be howling at the
moon.
Free spirited as the mustangs the can't be tamed.
Let's do this Peterpan....come take my hand and
let's follow our stand.

Wish apon a star and after the last word please
will you call out my name!

LenaSaunders

Poetic Ghost

Darkest hour has become the muse to bloom a
poetic flower. Words flowing so easily come
time three a.m.

Death of endearment has done taken its flight
and no longer am I putting up a fight.

True test is now where I need to be my best.
Round it up and drink from a full cup.

Last thing to be is stuck without a truck, oh
wait...mine was smashed and taken from me.
Now I am under strained pressure will I ever
even measure?

Do not think this has me down! I do not quit I
just fake a smile to all in town. I will be okay
one day and see again I am built this way.

Pressure builds quick and deep, in the darkness I
lay alone and silently weep.
Caspered to a ghost to become not even a
shadow.

Just catch me under the cover waiting for the
luck of my four leaf clover!

LenaSaunders

Breakdown

Lost from the visions of past deceptions running
fiercely through my mind.
Captured from the conformed battered childhood
of what was not spoke of.
The webs were disturbed when new blood was
victimized. Now the mind rewinds and revisits
everytime I close my eyes. Oh how I pray these
acient days would just fade away and leave my
mind to find better days to dream about.

LenaSaunders

Kick Dust

13

Wallowing in such pain and misery. Dooms will
pass, it's just a matter of time. No more catch
you later.
No more see you later, and no more I love yous.
I'm just a broken tool that has no more use.
So I'm tossed away to rust.
I might as well just kick the dust.

LenaSaunders

Mindwar

Sinking deeper and deeper into my mind and
seeing the things that need to be let go.
Trapped in the debilitating horror of my life's
descending quarrel.
Fighting every hour to beat how weak it makes
me.
Feeling as if the depression is overtaking me.
Just need one chance to make my exit from these
chains of haunting nightmares.
Paused on what has not yet seized from
crippling me.
No one knows all I have been through, no one
could know how to even handle my sorrow.
Some would deny me, some will turn away, and
others will say I am just a catastrophe.
I say this depression has its love on me.
Will I ever be set free of this failing
monstrosity?

LENASAUNDERS

Blended Youth

Youth years raised with a variety of characters
sheltered for short spurts of stays. There were
hippies, musicians, Becky home makers and
Enthusiasts. One would move out and we find a
new stray on the couch the next few days.

Learning how to live in such blended
environments became our second nature.
Not often we had a dull moment. Even when we
were sent to bed by eight we stole laughters
from the staircase.

Constant cooking varieties of breakfasts, snacks
and entrées to explore our taste buds. We
listened to different types of music with many
pickin and grinnin. Dancing around silly and
learning to feel the rythemic groove.

Those were days that I could enjoy freedom.
Those were the days our house had little privacy
or alone time. Those were the days that moms
helping others she would just meet, were my
peace of mind.

LenaSaunders

Ghastly Manifestation

Sitting here listening to great beats... inspiring in
so many ways. Or I may just be overthinking
things.
Jesters, Vikings, Gamers, Musicians, and Artists
of vast colors and skills, raking in all kinds of
wants and thrills.

Left dancing in the catacombs of the thoughts of
a night's unwind.
Speak out.. I could not!
Speak out... I would not!
Worried none of how unraveled one came
undone.

Salt to sting fresh open wounds as confidence
filled your space. Wondering why I kept my
back turned? Was to be unseen to what I could
not unsee.

Left me ghosted to froth in how unkind it
became.
Speak out...I could not!
Speak out...I would not!
Words of a writer escape me in your nearby
proximity.

Curiouser more is how I smile kindly to show;
How I rise to show no fear when you are near.
How I magically glow with scorpion charm,
even among vaporous arrogant foos.
How I can be alike a chameleon, and show
kaleidoscope views of the person I become from
that nights unwind.

Left me breathing a fighters mentality.
Speak out...I could not!
Speak out...I would not!
If you see me again, always remember
✹✹I am speaking very loudly✹✹
Soon...
You will hear me!

LenaSaunders

Pearl Coated

Sounds almost candy-coated!
Won't we hyme the chilling truth.

So to be clear. You claim she is a man hater!
Then she would be cleverly cold to castrate you
right there where you stand. For she is a man
eater, with her teasing siren mantra.

Truely blessed to hear this little one sing her
luring magic. Believe her when she says she's
has skills.

Not a man can handle such a mighty fierce
temptress. You will get blown away with
glistening titiful pearling.

Only allow two encounters for the third time
there will be no reckoning. For at the last
minutes hour she will have sang her spell deeply
in with her playful wiley ways.

To look apon her feverish auburn eyes you could
not disguise her infernos heat.

If your intent be true she will not think to defile
you. Now be your intent bring more negative
and harm, then you should be so very alarmed.

Cause honey,
She already has had her siren glock set on you!

©LenaSaunders
//Bean

Past, Present, Future

Not a test of who loves who
No contest of who cares more
No selfish thoughts of more needs than others
No forgotten bones just more monochromes

Teachings to be a better being
Taught to fight for the rights
Shown more for the undesired
Sights were set on being a bright light

Change brought on by forgotten words
Modifications were prayed for with tears
Advance with birth given fiction or facts
Reversal of blackened hearts bled from gray
fears

Taken apart from my woven ways
Test of time will be my future rhymes
Taste of true freedom in my future days
Tracing no path of the mountain climbs

Catch me next with terrific textures
Trust being mixed in a blender
Drank from my cup of different mixtures
Once I'm back, I will be the greatest defender

LenaSaunders❤

Front Line

Terrorized from minds unknown
Actions stale by feeble foundation
Knowing more than told
Experience gained from past living

Messy is unstable tranquility
Excellence is captured with organization

Awareness may seek what we need
Waste of time knowing the bottom line
Answers are there in front line
Yesteryears need to be all left behind!

LenaSaunders

Angel Wings

Angel Wings

(M)ountains of laughter brought from her personality.
(A)lways showed hospitality in many ways.
(R)ather spunky and spirited to the end.
(Y)es we will all miss you dearly. (F)lightless angle you are now free. (L)eaving behind the love you showered abroad.
(Y)ou are now home with God. (W)aiting at the gate will be all your loved ones past.
(I)n this moment we will remember your smiling face.
(T)ouched everyone's heart who met you
(H)ad us rolling on the floor.
(A)nother special lady has been hugged by God
(N)ot to worry we know you are out of pain.
(G)ave your family and friends memories that will carry in our hearts.
(E)ven heaven will see the best part of you.
(L)oving natured and funniest lady will now watch us from above.
(S)ing your heavenly song whispered from the cardinal letting those know your there and you are set free!

LenaSaunders

Winters Trace

Windy season is sweeping trees free of all
shedded leaves. Shows us winter is around the
corner.

Soon the snow will blanket the fields. Slushy
brown mush scooped to the sides. Burying cars
as they scrape by.

Chapped lips from the freezie breeze..nose
shines red as Rudolph the special reindeer.

Hot cocoa and home built fires are the best part
of winter year. If I had my wish I would be
away from all this stinging cold bitterness.

Aside from all that... There are memories to
make cookies and bake.

Jolly holly season brings magic aboard.
Thankful givings and families gathering for
festivities to embrace.

May even get a snowball or more thrown at your
arrival. Warning kids do play!

Santa's checking that list always twice, watch
your p's and q's his eyes are on you.
Are you naughty or nice?
Can we really say either way?
I would enjoy helping those elves working so
hard to bring joy to them all.

Nothing to giving, more when it's giving from
the heart. The best gifts have been crafted with
thought. Not a pretty penny spent at all to bring
a smile to a face.

That's the true Christmas trace.

LenaSaunders

Life's Unfold

25

Turn upside down and inside out
Pieces scattered all about
Ran as fast as Shazam

Absent from nights unwind
Got twisted away in ways unkind
Lifted above before impact

A brilliant young soul removed to be held
Forever twenty lives lived stands in front of the
lord
Smiling down knowing love showered him with
adore

Whispering heavenly words....
Daddy...Mommy, my brother too... love our
memories and smile more
Grandpa and the family has met me at the gate
I am home with warm embrace, dry the tear
trace
For every breath we take God has sealed our fate
It was my time, as short it was, you Blessed me
with unconditional loving grace

Swallowing back to not ask why
Time took away a special sweet guy
Remember as life unfolds sometimes distraction
comes without being told

LenaSaunders

Unreal

Farwell, calls you out to be no more. Pick
yourself up from the floor two.

Time after time unanswered calls ade to the
feelings that I'm pestering

Now stagnant talking is all thats left, the charm
has no reasons to be.

It seems ones life is to mundane and a bore life
is not living when waiting all day.

Memories had chances to be made,
Just to clear the air. The one who loved only saw
closed doors, concerts and pumpkin patches,
fairs and parties saw another's time to stake
precious memories...

Now the eyes of the soul truely sees...
No not you. No cant be true....
no not you Now the eyes of the soul knows you
were not ever the real one.

LenaSaunder

Memories Kept

I do need something you proof....
All I can do is see you...
You are all over...
All around me...
At the corner store , even in the bestroom.......

Oh please memories
never leave me...
I need to have them here always..
To never leave me....
All I can do is run from it..
Does not even help it...

There you are...
Even when I close my eyes...

Heart strings being pulled in major ways.
All I want is my memories to never leave me

Oh please memories..never leave me
I need to have them here always
To never leave me
All I can do is run from it
Does not even help it

There is no more fight left in me
I have tried in to many ways
You just will never see me
All I can do is run from it
Does not even help it.

Moon Phase

Moons phases has my energies in a real mess
I do confess!
Ups and downs..
Got all turned around
Been feeling like a sad lost clown
My frown is more upside right than upside down
I am trying to fix my crown
I just need more time to release some more of
the torment of my present life
My energy has faded to some greyish brown
drouted glaze
I just want to know that it will all be ok
Maybe even just normal one day

END Game

Dam another thinker and right now my thinker is back on a blunker.

Foggy brain clouds and spurts of rain.
Endless amounts of my own built misery lane.
Sorrows today deserts tomorrow.
"Every Storm Runs out of Rain" .
Tragic comes from those storms brought with such blunt force
Killing all energy source
These storms so powerful
Left behind wreckage of all debris
Damaged and fractured to the core.
Weak is not weak, only fallen from unbearable weight.
Do you know that weak is the strongest ones of them all.
Down and out gives strength to live.
Sometimes will even show clarity where doubt once lived.
Doubt pecked and pecked calling my shame as if I was only to blame.
Things I've done wrong I have tried to right, said I am sorry.

Expect no forgiveness only asked how to make right
Things I have not said sorry for are done to serve as a rue to expose the abuse.
Yes I have used and cheated, lied and drama created, a jester of some a master of my own chaos
I assure you for over a year I knew more than you knew. Only evidence couldn't be had to let what be... Be
Soon the cookies and candy laid to intice or bring strife would bring my plan to an end.

The constant target sinking back attack with hate your aim game.
Lovely hand played
Please don't remember my name.
End game!

Point of View

A friendship becomes a friendship near or far, no matter what color you are.

Talking to strangers in the cyber-land is a risky thing indeed. Provokes false catfishing in 76% of who you see. Fake world we live and breath. Fake is at least one when looked all 4 ways.

Catch me catch me says the gingerbread man. You can't catch me says ginger B, I run as fast as panthers you see. Ginger B fell from her dwell and claws away to free from her hell.

Do not tell

Why not tell it if l am not a wicked mockery. Make me a star of the circus show. Find me reading all your true intentions to break me.

Catch me catch me I'm the gingerbread man. You cant catch me I'm onioned out spiderically stacked for constant moving attacks. Snack on all the 1000001 binary cyber whacks!